THE
CAREER
DESIGN
MAP

Published by Contempus Leadership LLC
177 Huntington Avenue, Suite 1703 #483763
Boston, MA 02115

Authored by Daniel Freehling

ISBN: 979-8-9876542-0-0

THE
CAREER DESIGN MAP

To my coach, Amy Ruppert Donovan, for encouraging me to write this book, and my wife, Heather Staats-Freehling, for being my thought partner throughout the process.

TABLE OF CONTENTS

ACKNOWLEDGMENTS

Thanks to all who provided their feedback, expertise, and support during the writing process. Special thanks to:

Heather Staats-Freehling, for always being there for me and for your integral contributions to the book.

Amy Ruppert Donovan, of The Integreship Group, for all you've done for me personally and to build the coaching profession's next generation of leaders.

My parents, Jim and Nancy Freehling, and my brother, Nick Freehling, for your unconditional support and gracious listening throughout the writing process.

My professors and classmates at the George Washington University for the opportunity to explore much of the leadership research and theory underpinning the concepts in this book, especially to Dr. Michael Pobát for advising my independent study.

Sonja Whipp, for your creative consulting on the engaging stories for each chapter.

Genny Boscardin, for taking my words and designing the imaginative map illustration.

Karen Alber, of The Integreship Group, for your thoughtful early readthrough and suggestions.

Danielle Anderson, of Ink Worthy Books, for your outstanding developmental editing.

Kevin Thai, of Three Circles Studio, for capturing the author headshot.

Emily Fritz, Casey Fritz, and the rest of the team at Albatross Book Co., for your striking cover design and other expertise in helping me bring the book through the finish line.

My wonderful colleagues at EnCompass LLC, for your continuous support in pursuing my career aspirations.

My coaching clients, for allowing me to refine these concepts with you and for your ongoing trust in working together.

INTRODUCTION

GO TO THESE SCHOOLS. Join these professions. Stay in your unrewarding job. Keep your head down. Climb the corporate ladder. Someday, you might even become the top dog. Then you can retire with enough time and money to do what you really want.

Despite being obviously limiting and outdated, this message still underlies much of the career and leadership advice out there from family, friends, coworkers, and even supposed experts.

I'm a coach who partners with today's top rising leaders to challenge this conventional narrative, create the careers they really want, and lead their way.

For all its faults, the old-school system brought a certain sense of comfort and security. If you followed proven paths and worked hard, you could be reasonably sure you'd be able to provide a decent life for yourself and your family.

Of course, as entire industries are upended and once-lucrative jobs fall victim to massive layoffs, it's clear this is less and less the case. Although it can be tempting to follow the well-intentioned guidance of those who came before, it won't serve you in the long run.

My clients understand this. They intuitively see that the economy is in the late stages of a fundamental shift away from the industrial era. That future success requires greater focus on differentiation and agility than standardization and control. That the role of a leader is to bring people together to take on important challenges. That meaning matters more than ever for their own engagement and that of their colleagues.

They know that as the pace of change continues to accelerate, they must be highly adaptable. That what they do for work in ten years may not even exist yet. That inflexible planning is out, and design thinking and experimentation are in.

At the same time, they rightly want to act with intention rather than letting the wind take them where it will. Inevitably, it leads to the question, "What, then, am I supposed to do?"

The answer, in brief, is that navigating a meaningful, modern career is exactly that: navigating. It's more personal, complex, and hands-on than before. It requires setting a direction, taking action, and adjusting your course as you gain greater insight and conditions change. It demands proceeding without perfect information and embracing continuous learning along the way. As such, it calls not for a step-by-step playbook but for a map.

That's why I created the Career Design Map. It is a powerful framework to help you get your bearings and chart your own course in this emerging reality. Now, I want to share it with you.

Although the concepts in this book are universally applicable, they are particularly essential for my fellow Millennials and the incoming Gen Z workforce as we face career-shaping decisions in a rapidly changing world.

Visit CareerDesignQuiz.com to take the free quiz. Then, use the chapters of this book to interpret your results and put them into practice.

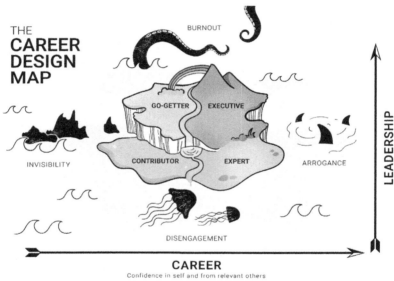

THE
**CAREER
DESIGN
MAP**

BURNOUT

GO-GETTER EXECUTIVE

INVISIBILITY

CONTRIBUTOR EXPERT

ARROGANCE

DISENGAGEMENT

CAREER
Confidence in self and from relevant others

LEADERSHIP
Enabling people to achieve a common purpose

1
THE CAREER DESIGN MAP

WITHOUT FURTHER ADO, here is the Career Design Map. It provides a starting point and ongoing reference for understanding and addressing many of the crucial career and leadership questions of our time.

Why am I feeling so burned out? Why am I not finding my work fulfilling? Why do I keep getting overlooked for opportunities? How do I increase my earning power? Am I falling behind the curve or still growing? Am I working to live or living to work? How do I reach my full potential as a leader?

The Career Design Map allows you to zoom out from the day-to-day and see the big picture of your current and desired career advancement and leadership levels.

INTERPRETING THE MAP: CAREER

The Career Design Map defines career, shown on the x-axis, as "confidence in self and from relevant others." Regardless of your line of work, career growth is a function of both your self-assurance and trust from stakeholders. You can't get what you don't ask for, as they say, but you also won't be given something just because you ask for it.

In a traditional job, your promotions and raises are driven by putting yourself forward for higher-level opportunities and your organization's confidence in your ability to perform. When applying for a new position, it's up to you to explain how you will deliver value and for those on the hiring side to believe you. For freelancers and entrepreneurs, your career success is created by engaging with customers and investors and these stakeholders responding in kind.

Even as helpful technology makes it easier than ever to find online job postings, submit applications, and promote yourself on social media, career advancement comes down to your relationships. In a world of noise, your reputation matters more than your résumé. Building self-confidence, earning trust, and proving your unique value-add are the best ways to position yourself for lasting career success.

INTERPRETING THE MAP: LEADERSHIP

The Career Design Map defines leadership, represented on the y-axis, as "enabling people to achieve a common purpose." From sports coaches striving to win a championship to civil rights figures working to change a nation, leaders bring people together toward a collective aim.

The task of the modern leader is no longer to have all the answers and tell others what to do. Rather, it entails promoting collaboration and innovation. Positioning people to do better work than they thought possible. Supporting them in reaching their highest potential. Acting with integrity, responsibility, and wisdom. Empowering teams to thrive in change. By doing so, leaders cultivate environments that drive long-term results.

Like with career, even with so much technological change, leadership is more about people than ever before. Sometimes leadership means inspiring others with a compelling vision; other times, it means trusting people to run with their own ideas. Sometimes it calls for opening space for discussion and debate; other times, it calls for making the tough decisions needed to move forward. The key is that leadership is not a solo act; it requires engaging with others on something that matters.

THE DANGEROUS SEAS & THE MEANINGFUL FOUR

In sharp contrast to both the "hustle and grind" and "quiet quitting" fads, the Career Design Map takes a real-world, balanced approach to career and leadership. Too high or low on either axis and you're in the Dangerous Seas of Invisibility, Arrogance, Disengagement, and Burnout. The Dangerous Seas, explained in Part I of the book, are the extremes of career and leadership you need to watch out for.

Within the bounds of the Dangerous Seas, it's up to you to build your career your way. To help you organize your thinking, the Career Design Map's idyllic land consists of the Meaningful Four: Contributor, Go-Getter, Expert, and Executive. The Meaningful Four, explored in Part II of the book, are the broad categories of fulfilling, successful careers.

The Career Design Map holds that impactful leadership

toward an important purpose (the Executive quadrant) is the highest form of career and leadership excellence. At the same time, any of the other Meaningful Four are entirely reasonable options to choose. You have to decide how much you want to prioritize career and leadership in your own life.

Think of it like the interconnected concepts of diet and exercise. Although eating healthily and being in great shape are the highest forms of these areas, it's perfectly okay if these are not the top priorities for you.

Even if you don't eat a full-fledged Mediterranean diet and compete in triathlons, it's wise to avoid the extremes of undereating, overeating, inactivity, or overtraining.

Each of the following chapters explains a section of the map with a story inspired by real-world examples and provides strategic considerations and an exercise to put what you learn into practice.

As you read through each chapter, ask where you currently see yourself. Where do you want to go? What will you do to move in that direction?

The path from where you are to where you want to be will rarely be a straight line. Your desired direction will shift over time with changing life circumstances and as your interests and goals evolve. You will invariably encounter detours, setbacks, failures, and new insights along the way. When you know where you are and where you want to be, however, you can begin to take focused action.

If you haven't already, visit CareerDesignQuiz.com to take the free quiz.

Let's get started.

PART I
THE DANGEROUS SEAS

2
INVISIBILITY

"AT LEAST THEY GOT BACK TO ME," Mike muttered to himself as he read yet another rejection email in his inbox. Truth be told, he was pleasantly surprised. He frequently didn't hear anything at all from the black hole of online applications.

Mike has been on the job hunt for nearly a year after graduating from college. He isn't really sure what he wants to do next, so he has been sporadically applying to any online job openings he finds.

He thinks he might want to be a product manager at a tech company. After all, that's what his older cousin is doing, and she seems to like it. Or maybe he wants to do something with marketing. He didn't mind that class in his business program.

"It's just impossible to get noticed these days, especially for someone like me," he thought as he scanned the job board listings for the fourth time that afternoon, hoping against hope that one of these applications would finally be the one.

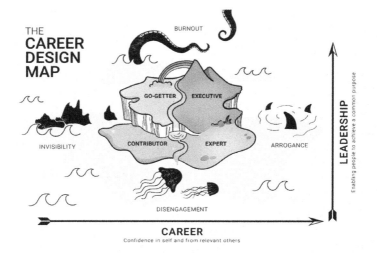

THE
**CAREER
DESIGN
MAP**

BURNOUT

GO-GETTER EXECUTIVE

CONTRIBUTOR EXPERT

INVISIBILITY

ARROGANCE

DISENGAGEMENT

LEADERSHIP
Enabling people to achieve a common purpose

CAREER
Confidence in self and from relevant others

STRATEGIC CONSIDERATIONS

Mike is experiencing invisibility, which results from too little confidence in himself and from relevant stakeholders. He hasn't taken the actions over time to build his self-assurance, and those on the hiring end are not confident in his ability to do the job successfully. As a result, Mike is getting increasingly frustrated with the process and wonders why he isn't having any luck.

If you're experiencing invisibility, you need to advance your career by building your own confidence and that of those who matter for your success. Reflect on and clarify what you want to do in your next role, refine your story for why you would be a good hire, pick up relevant volunteer or internship experience, conduct informational interviews with people you admire, and educate yourself on the industry so you can present yourself well.

DANGERS: Staying in invisibility or focusing on leadership before career. Whether you're in a low-level role or on the job hunt, being in invisibility is not the time to be humble and shy. No one is noticing you. You need to work up the courage to start putting yourself out there right away.

OPPORTUNITIES: Becoming a contributor or a go-getter. By taking action to build trust in others, you can move into these meaningful career types. From there, you will be better positioned to become an expert or executive if you'd like to move in those directions.

EXERCISE: JUST ONE CONVERSATION

When I used to volunteer as a coach for college students and work with early career clients, they were often overwhelmed at the prospect of networking. It brought up uncomfortable connotations of shaking hands and slapping backs in a hotel ballroom.

Instead of going to a career fair or networking event, identify just one person you find interesting and whose work you'd like to learn more about. That's right, just one person. You can really do it.

- Reach out (preferably have someone introduce you) and ask if they would be willing to meet with you for a brief informational chat to learn more about their career.

- Be absolutely sure you aren't approaching this conversation transactionally. The purpose is not to ask them about openings at their company or to put you in touch with someone who is hiring. People will shut down in that case.

- Ask about their career path, their thoughts on trends in their field, and interesting types of jobs and organizations you should consider. Talk about your long- and short-term goals and ask any questions you have.

- Let your curiosity and research shine. Sincerely thank them for their time and ask if there's anyone else they would be willing to connect you with for a similar chat.

3
ARROGANCE

"WON'T WORK!" The senior management team sat in stunned silence.

A rising star at the company had just laid out an exciting and rock-solid business case for adopting a new technology and shifting to a new market. "I've seen it all—been there, done that—and this won't work," Barbara, a VP at the company, continued, providing no evidence or rationale to support her defiant stance. The CEO and CFO exchanged knowing glances.

They had become increasingly worried over the past few years that Barbara, although quite accomplished, was now standing in the way of progress and "kicking down" in a flailing attempt to protect herself. Her business unit's performance had begun to falter, and although she blamed the market, everyone knew it was because she refused to listen, adapt, and change.

Years ago, she was considered next in line to succeed the CEO, but most stakeholders had since soured on that. This meeting was the final nail in the coffin. The CEO would ask for her resignation later that month.

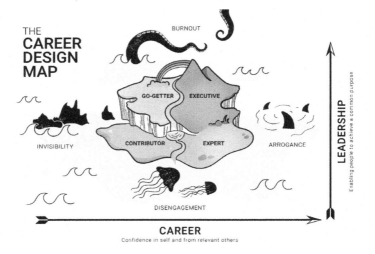

STRATEGIC CONSIDERATIONS

Barbara is experiencing arrogance, which results from overconfidence in herself and from those around her. She hasn't listened to honest feedback in years and has shut down people who've tried to provide constructive criticism.

Barbara is surrounded by "yes people." She is actively harming her own future and that of her organization by dismissing fresh ideas. Her career success is now working against her.

If you're in arrogance, you need to actively reduce your overconfidence and remove yourself from the bubble of others' overconfidence.

Arrogance is often the most surprising and difficult Dangerous Sea to find yourself in. If you've received this result on the quiz or think you're in it from your interpretation of the map, know that it isn't a value judgment or permanent situation but a warning sign. Many highly successful people will veer into arrogance at some point in their careers. The important point is to accept this and take action to walk yourself back.

DANGERS: Staying in arrogance or focusing on leadership instead of career. This is not the time to worry about bringing people together to work toward a common purpose. You're not thinking objectively and are being told what you want to hear from those around you. Fix this by actively reducing your over-confidence and surrounding yourself with truth-tellers.

OPPORTUNITIES: Moving back into being an expert or executive. Once you can honestly assess yourself and trust the feedback you are receiving, you can return to making your best individual and leadership contributions.

EXERCISE: FOSTERING A LEARNING MINDSET

- Identify one area in which you'd like to learn and grow. Think of a person you know who excels in your selected area. Ask if they would be willing to mentor (or even "reverse mentor") you.

- Come up with a challenging project you'd like to work on.

- Ask your mentor for advice and resources. Shadow them to learn from their approach. Seek critical feedback from them along the way.

- Reflect on the learning process. Where have you made progress? Where are you struggling? How can you use this experience to increase your humility and foster a learning mindset in other areas of your life and work?

4

DISENGAGEMENT

"WE ARE A VALUES-DRIVEN ORGANIZATION that seeks excellence in all we do."

The facilitator read the words aloud from the flip chart toward the end of the all-day visioning retreat in the eighth-floor conference room of One Corporate Drive.

Bill turned his head to the side in a deft maneuver to simultaneously sneak a peek of the wall clock and roll his eyes without anyone noticing. "Who cares about this?" he thought to himself. "Why does it matter?"

Bill had been fascinated with science and technology since he was a kid. He studied chemistry in college and loved to restore antique cars as a hobby. He had taken a job in laboratory instrument sales when he graduated and, ten years later, was still doing the same thing.

His curiosity had faded more than his buzz from the hazelnut coffee from the afternoon break. At least his college football team was at home this weekend; that was something to look forward to.

THE
**CAREER
DESIGN
MAP**

BURNOUT

GO-GETTER   EXECUTIVE

INVISIBILITY   CONTRIBUTOR   EXPERT   ARROGANCE

DISENGAGEMENT

LEADERSHIP
Enabling people to achieve a common purpose

CAREER
Confidence in self and from relevant others

STRATEGIC CONSIDERATIONS

Bill is experiencing disengagement, which results from too little buy-in for enabling others to achieve a common purpose. Being in disengagement is a continuous draining of energy. Bill frequently thinks about getting a new job but is so demoralized he hesitates to make it happen.

Disengagement is an indicator that Bill isn't finding meaning in his work. It can be a defense mechanism against being a poor fit for the work itself or the workplace environment. It's a sign you're in the wrong role or organization and need to find a better match for your interests.

If you're in disengagement, you need to increase your leadership by finding a purpose you believe in and working with others toward achieving it.

DANGERS: Staying in disengagement or focusing on career before leadership. You won't get out of disengagement by going after a higher-level job or trying to make more money. Instead, you need to intentionally find a better fit that allows you to be part of something that matters to you.

OPPORTUNITIES: Becoming a contributor or an expert. Once you identify a role and organization working toward something meaningful to you, you can begin to feel good about your efforts and involvement.

EXERCISE: BUILD A ROLE FILTER

Reflect on a time you were fully engaged in a personal or professional project. Perhaps you were even in a state of "flow."

What did it feel like to work on the project? What does your engagement with the project reveal about what you're good at? What does it show about what energizes you? What does it demonstrate about what you care about?

- Write these answers down, then reflect on them to find throughlines and patterns.

- Synthesize the throughlines and patterns into a role filter: a list of three to five key features of a position and environment that would be a better fit for you.

  » For example, Bill's car hobby may reveal he would enjoy a role with such elements as being tasked with solving discrete challenges, diving deep into research, and showcasing his work to a community of peers.

- Is it possible to shift into such a role within your current organization? If not, you need to look elsewhere. A promotion, raise, or getting yourself into the same situation at another firm won't do the trick here. Use the role filter as your guide when searching for and evaluating new opportunities.

5
BURNOUT

"I REALLY NEED TO GET TO BED." It had just turned 2:00 a.m., and Nia was exhausted.

She was a passionate advocate for education reform and cared deeply about the cause of the nonprofit at which she worked. Her team had recently lost several staff members, and Nia felt at times like she was personally holding the organization together.

She was talking with the principal at one of their partner schools and heard some families were having trouble paying for their kids to attend the eagerly awaited junior class trip to Costa Rica. Despite already working more than full-time, Nia took it upon herself to help. She reached out to her network and found the perfect grant opportunity.

It was due later in the week, and the funding would cover the cost of the trip for the entire class. She wrapped up the draft to submit the proposal first thing in the morning and closed her laptop for the eighth late night in a row.

On her way to work four hours later, she stopped by her usual coffee shop. "That would be nice," she thought, imagining the joy of the barista being able to clock out after his shift and not have his phone pinging with emails around the clock. She realized her job had become unsustainable and she needed to make a change, but there was too much work to do to stop now.

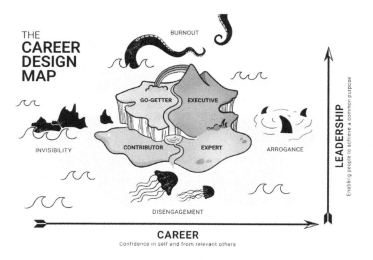

THE
CAREER
DESIGN
MAP

BURNOUT

GO-GETTER   EXECUTIVE

INVISIBILITY   CONTRIBUTOR   EXPERT   ARROGANCE

DISENGAGEMENT

CAREER
Confidence in self and from relevant others

LEADERSHIP
Enabling people to achieve a common purpose

STRATEGIC CONSIDERATIONS

Nia is experiencing burnout, which is caused by unsustainably high dedication to enabling others to achieve a common purpose. Burnout results from too much leadership (yes, you read that right). It is fundamentally the opposite of disengagement, though the two are frequently confused.

Nia is putting the needs of others above her own well-being. It is a dangerous position for her mental health and the quality of her relationships.

If you're in burnout, you need to actively decrease your leadership by setting boundaries. This will allow you to lead in a sustainable manner over the long term. Leadership is a lifelong endeavor, not a quick sprint or even a grueling marathon.

DANGERS: Staying in burnout or focusing on career advancement before setting boundaries on your leadership. Getting a promotion or taking a new job isn't an automatic solution for burnout. People are often chronically burned out and carry their overcommitment across roles and organizations. If you're in burnout, you need to set boundaries right away, especially when it feels like you can't or everything will fall apart.

OPPORTUNITIES: Returning to being a go-getter or executive. By pulling back to leading at a sustainably high pace, you will better serve your team, organization, and cause.

EXERCISE: TAKE TIME|DELEGATE|ADVOCATE

Burnout often feels overwhelming. Take these three concrete actions to start setting boundaries and free up space to think clearly about your next steps.

- **TAKE TIME**: Schedule an entire day off. Move or cancel your meetings for that day and remain completely offline.

- **DELEGATE**: Delegate (if you're able) or ask someone for help on one project or task they'd be better positioned to take on.

- **ADVOCATE**: Advocate for additional staff, consultants, vendors, or technology that would alleviate your overwork.

PART II
THE MEANINGFUL FOUR

6
CONTRIBUTOR

"TIME TO EAT!" yelled John as he pulled five of his famous cheeseburgers off the grill.

John was a senior accounts payable specialist and was loving his company's new Summer Fridays policy. He had spent his Friday off squeezing in an early morning round of golf with his buddies before coaching his oldest's baseball team. He even managed to make a quick afternoon trip to the beach with his wife, Emily.

"Any word on the new boss?" Emily asked, knowing John had been offered the finance manager role but declined. "They picked someone. He seems like a decent guy. I'll help him get up to speed when he starts next week."

John closed the lid to the grill and shut off the propane tank. "Time to eat!" he bellowed again, prompting the kids to finally leave the sprinkler and make their way to the patio.

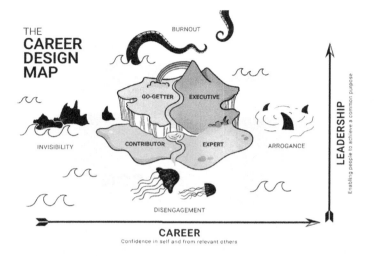

THE
**CAREER
DESIGN
MAP**

BURNOUT

GO-GETTER   EXECUTIVE

CONTRIBUTOR   EXPERT

INVISIBILITY   ARROGANCE

DISENGAGEMENT

LEADERSHIP
Enabling people to achieve a common purpose

CAREER
Confidence in self and from relevant others

STRATEGIC CONSIDERATIONS

John is a contributor. He cares enough about his work to responsibly do his job and be there for his team, but career advancement and leadership are not especially important to him.

He prioritizes spending his time elsewhere, with family and friends, volunteering, and on his hobbies.

John does good work and is satisfied where he is. He isn't particularly interested in rising through the ranks or becoming a sought-after expert. John's work life is generally low-stress and allows plenty of time for things that matter to him.

DANGERS: Devolving into invisibility or disengagement. Contributors need to be sure they continue to enjoy their jobs and remain committed and integral team members.

OPPORTUNITIES: Becoming a go-getter or an expert. With the trust and knowledge gained from being conscientious team players, contributors are well-positioned to step up as leaders or hone highly specialized skills.

EXERCISE: FROM TEAM PLAYER TO GO-GETTER OR EXPERT

Contributors have a lot to offer by becoming go-getters or experts. They often have a better view of an organization's opportunities and challenges than higher-ups and are well-positioned to make a difference.

Ask yourself the following questions, then decide if you want to make any changes.

- What recurring challenges do I see at my organization that leadership doesn't seem to notice?

- What new initiatives or improvements would make a real difference in the experience of our employees, clients, and customers?

- What steps could I take to become even better at what I do?

7

GO-GETTER

"I GOT INPUT FROM EVERYONE ON THE TEAM and put together a presentation for our meeting."

Isabella's boss, Lisa, was pleased but not surprised as she looked through the outstanding slide deck. Lisa knew Isabella was excited about the chance to collaborate more closely with the esteemed policy institute they were meeting with in a few weeks. Lisa had never asked her to prepare anything, but Isabella went ahead anyway.

Isabella had studied international relations as an undergraduate and gone on for a master's in conflict resolution. She is quite knowledgeable about the matter to be discussed.

Isabella has been working as a program associate at her organization for the past two years. She has excelled in her role, built relationships at all levels, and has continuously gone above and beyond to make the team better.

"Why don't you take the lead in presenting, Isabella?" asked Lisa.

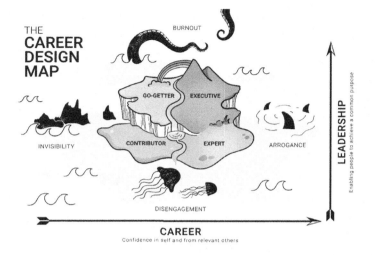

THE
**CAREER
DESIGN
MAP**

BURNOUT

GO-GETTER · EXECUTIVE

INVISIBILITY · CONTRIBUTOR · EXPERT · ARROGANCE

DISENGAGEMENT

CAREER
Confidence in self and from relevant others

LEADERSHIP
Enabling people to achieve a common purpose

STRATEGIC CONSIDERATIONS

Isabella is a go-getter. She is leading more than would be expected of someone in her position. She sincerely cares about the organization's purpose and takes it upon herself to enable others to succeed.

As a go-getter, your leadership exceeds your career advancement. It can be both a frustrating and exciting time. Isabella knows she is capable of more and is considering what's next.

Owning your core responsibilities and taking the initiative on stretch projects that help the team is the fastest way to prove yourself for greater leadership opportunities.

DANGERS: Falling into invisibility or burnout. Go-getters need to be sure they're going above and beyond selectively. Pick projects that solve real problems for the organization and receive the recognition they deserve. Be careful to not overextend yourself on thankless administrative tasks in your desire to support the team.

OPPORTUNITIES: Becoming an expert or executive. Being a go-getter is typically a transitory stage. Go-getters can take the expert path by engaging in more technical work or the executive path by focusing on their leadership development.

EXERCISE: I'M READY BECAUSE . . .

Go-getters need to build their own confidence and that of stakeholders to advance. Why aren't you currently the next level up in your organization or at another firm?

- Draw a line vertically down the middle of a piece of paper.

- Label the left side "I'm not ready because . . ." Under that label, write out all the reasons you don't think you can be at the next level. For example, "I can't because I'm too young," "I can't because I don't have a PhD," or "I can't because I don't have X years of experience."

- Go through the left side and cross out anything you can't change. For anything you can change, ask yourself how you might mitigate that deficit.

- Then, label the right side "I'm ready because . . ." Under that label, write out all the reasons you deserve to be at the next level. If you can't come up with these on your own, ask trusted friends and colleagues.

- Go through the right side. How can you demonstrate and communicate each of these assets to relevant decision-makers?

8
EXPERT

"YOU KNOW THIS WORK BETTER THAN ANYONE, MARIA.
We couldn't have closed this without you." Maria's boss raised a glass at the hotel bar. "To Maria!"

"To Maria!" the table echoed. Ice-cold liquor splashed onto everyone's hands as martinis and old fashioneds collided in midair. Maria was a force to be reckoned with. As sharp as she is funny, she had nailed the presentation earlier that day.

She had been preparing for weeks, anticipating every potential objection and rehearsing her talking points as if she was about to deliver the State of the Union.

Maria won over a tough client, impressing and reassuring them with her profound technical know-how, and secured millions in new business for her communications firm.

THE
**CAREER
DESIGN
MAP**

BURNOUT

GO-GETTER   EXECUTIVE

INVISIBILITY   CONTRIBUTOR   EXPERT   ARROGANCE

DISENGAGEMENT

CAREER
Confidence in self and from relevant others

LEADERSHIP
Enabling people to achieve a common purpose

STRATEGIC CONSIDERATIONS

Maria is an expert. She is highly skilled and valuable to the organization. She has spent years honing her craft through work assignments, formal education, and self-study. Maria is excellent at what she does. She is self-assured yet constantly learning and improving.

Maria is more of an individual contributor than a leader. Her success relies primarily on her personal effort and knowledge. Maria is well-compensated and respected as a top-notch performer.

DANGERS: Slipping into arrogance or disengagement. Experts need to be careful of their success going to their heads or becoming too far removed from their organization's purpose.

OPPORTUNITIES: Becoming an executive. The shift from technical expertise to higher levels of leadership is one of the most common yet challenging transitions. It requires changing your focus from your personal performance to enabling those around you to succeed.

EXERCISE: WORK THROUGH OTHERS

Look back at your calendar for the past two weeks. Roughly calculate how much time you spent on individual contributor tasks (in which you directly did the work) and how much time you spent on leadership tasks (in which you empowered others to do the work).

- What is the proportion of each? Where do you want it to be?

- Set a specific goal (write it down) for the next month to spend less time individually contributing and more time leading, if that's your desired direction.

- In a month, assess your progress and set another goal until you've reached your ideal balance between individual contributor and leader.

9

EXECUTIVE

"WHAT NEW IDEAS DO YOU HAVE? How can we expand what's working? Where can we be doing better? What would make a real difference?"

Alyssa asked question after question at the all-hands meeting. She was just the person you wanted in charge of the hospital at this time.

She had been honing her skills as a healthcare leader for years, successfully taking on multiple challenging roles across organizations and departments. Alyssa is highly respected in the field and the local community.

At the onset of the pandemic, Alyssa worked quickly with leaders at all levels in the hospital to stabilize the situation and communicate with patients, families, and employees. Now, she is looking for ways to involve the staff in improving care even more and generating innovative ideas.

"You're the closest to the patients, and we want to hear from you," she continued. Everyone from doctors to nurses to custodians excitedly stepped up to the microphones to add to the discussion.

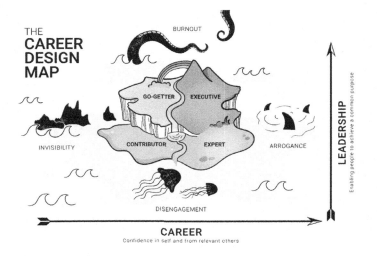

THE **CAREER DESIGN MAP**

BURNOUT

LEADERSHIP
Enabling people to achieve a common purpose

GO-GETTER EXECUTIVE

INVISIBILITY CONTRIBUTOR EXPERT ARROGANCE

DISENGAGEMENT

CAREER
Confidence in self and from relevant others

STRATEGIC CONSIDERATIONS

Alyssa is an executive. She is a powerful leader and is recognized as such. She uses her seat at the table to enable the people in her organization to achieve their common purpose.

Being an executive is when your leadership and career advancement are commensurately high. It's the pinnacle of leadership and career success and represents the greatest opportunity to make a major impact.

Simply having a high-level title does not make you a true executive. As we're painfully aware, many in C-suite positions would not fall into this quadrant of the Career Design Map.

DANGERS: Devolving into arrogance or burnout. Executives need to demonstrate day in and day out that they care about bringing out people's best to move the cause forward. There is a constant danger of falling behind the times, becoming defensive, or overextending yourself that you must guard against.

OPPORTUNITIES: Making a positive impact in the world. Executives have the opportunity to build something bigger than themselves, drive progress on important initiatives, and leave a lasting legacy.

EXERCISE: YOUR RETIREMENT CELEBRATION

Imagine it's your retirement party.

- How many people are there? Who has made a special trip for it? Who have you impacted throughout your career who couldn't be there?

- What are people saying about how you've made a difference in a cause you care about? An organization? Their careers? Their lives? The world?

- How satisfied are you with this? What, if anything, do you wish was different?

- What changes, if any, do you want to make as a result of this exercise?

10

THE HARD WORK

THE CAREER DESIGN MAP helps you see the forest for the trees in a new and often confusing era of career and leadership.

It contextualizes some of the major issues of our time. Despite tremendous opportunity available, some people remain frustratingly invisible. Other seemingly visionary leaders have achieved what appeared to be amazing success, only for it to be revealed that their arrogance blinded them and their organizations to reality.

Some people are so invested in their roles they are in danger of burnout, while others are hungry for a deeper connection to their work.

The Career Design Map and its accompanying quiz are not intended to be exact instruments. No tools can fully capture your unique situation. If you feel you are at a different point on the map or want to go in a different direction than your quiz answers indicate, adjust as necessary.

If you're ready to seriously begin making change, write down and reflect on your answers to the following questions. Then debrief, make a flexible plan, and start taking action, preferably with a trusted coach or at least an astute family member, friend, colleague, or mentor by your side.

In closing, my sincerest hope is that the Career Design Map has given you permission to challenge conventional advice and start creating the career you really want. Now that you've read the book, the hard work begins.

REFLECTION QUESTIONS:

- Where am I now on the Career Design Map?

- How satisfied am I with that?

- In which direction do I want to move?

- What excites me about that direction?

- What do I fear will hold me back from moving in that direction?

- What do I already do well that I could build on to move in that direction?

- What changes to my mindsets, behaviors, and habits would make the biggest difference in moving me in that direction?

- What additional experience, education, and connections would help move me in that direction?

- Who could I speak with who has successfully taken a similar journey?

- Am I really ready to commit to moving in that direction starting today? If not, what is holding me back?

- What questions are still on my mind?

ABOUT THE AUTHOR

 **DAN FREEHLING** is a leadership and career coach and the founder of Contempus Leadership LLC. He partners with fellow rising leaders directly and through forward-looking organizations seeking to develop their leadership pipeline. Dan deeply understands his clients' challenges and informs his practice with substantial experience and education in the latest in organizational leadership and coaching.

He has led highly rated, multimillion-dollar organizational and leadership development contracts, overseen a worldwide leadership coaching program, and personally coached purpose-driven leaders at the manager, director, and vice president levels.

Dan holds an MA in Organizational Leadership & Learning from the George Washington University, an MBA from the University of Massachusetts Amherst, and a BA in International Relations and Political Science from Boston University.

MORE INFORMATION ON WORKING TOGETHER CAN BE FOUND AT

contempusleadership.com.

Made in United States
North Haven, CT
26 April 2023

35933026R00037